LEARN AND GROW
SUSTAINABLY

A Lesson Plan Series for Grades 3-5

LEARN AND GROW
SUSTAINABLY

A Lesson Plan Series for Grades 3-5

by Gina Riggio

Habitable Press

Acknowledgments:

We thank Brendan Mullan, Amanda Joy, Chris Butch, Diane Keller, and Anne McHugh for providing invaluable feedback in the review and editing of this lesson plan series. We also gratefully acknowledge Daniel Klock and Reba Paul for designing and testing the GreenSpace Sunflower Grow Kit.

GreenSpace is a permaculture center that provides Pennsylvania and Delaware with nutritious and ethically grown produce. GreenSpace applies the latest research in sustainable agriculture to enable efficient urban farming and develop experimental practices for long-term human spaceflight. To learn more, visit http://growgreenspace.org/

Printed in the United States of America
Second Printing: June 2018
First Printing: May 2017

Published by Habitable Press
1001 4th Ave, Suite 3201, Seattle WA 98154
http://habitablepress.org/

ISBN-10: 978-0692878842
ISBN-13: 069287884X

Table of Contents

About This Workbook

The purpose of Learn and Grow Sustainably is to teach students of all ages to appreciate the interaction between humans, plants, and the environment. Our Sunflower Grow Kit is fully compostable and allows students to witness the growth of an edible food product within 10 days. This lesson plan series will help students to learn about plant growth, nutrition, and physiology as well as a little bit of materials science through experiments on our kit's compostable plastic container. These topics are important for fostering a sense of environmental stewardship for a more sustainable future.

The activities in this two part lesson series are optimized for grades 3-5 and are aligned with the science standards for that grade band. However, this lesson can be adapted to suit K-2, Middle School, High School, and Adult Education by aligning the lessons to similar standards at different grade levels. If you are an outreach coordinator or a college instructor, we hope that you will find these lessons useful for your students as well. Please feel free to contact us if you have any questions about this process. We have found the online searchable version of the Next Generation Science Standards to be invaluable for aligning our content modern science education methods, which can be found at http://www.nextgenscience.org/search-standards

We developed the lessons in this series to accompany the Sunflower Microgreen Grow Kit, which is available through our website, at farmers' markets and local businesses in the area, and Amazon.com. Below is the web address to purchase kits. Please contact us directly if you are interested in placing an order greater than 50 kits.

https://www.growgreenspace.org/growkit/

If you have used our lesson plans and want to share your results with us or let us know about your creative adaptations to our work, please share it on our twitter page by using the following account name and hashtag:

@growgreenspace and #MyGrowKit

Thank you for giving our lesson plans a try! We hope you and your students enjoy them!

All the best,

Lesson 1
The Five Needs of Plants

In this activity, students will learn about what plants need to grow by using the Sunflower Grow Kit as a model. They will experience the complete life cycle of a plant and have the opportunity to see the role that each of the five needs plays, demonstrating the crosscutting concept of cause and effect.

Introduction to the Five Needs of Plants

Plants Need Air

Plants need air to be healthy. A common misconception is that plants get everything they need from the soil. In fact, all of the carbon that the plant uses to make its body structure comes from the **carbon dioxide** in the air. Plants inhale the carbon dioxide that we exhale, and exhale **oxygen** that we need to survive. Our relationship to plants is close and important. Without plants, we would have an unbreathable atmosphere.

Plants Need Water

Plants need water to keep their **stems** and **leaves** crisp. However, too much water is also dangerous as it can cause the roots to rot and the plant to become limp. Water is also essential for plants to deliver **nutrients** from their roots up through the stems, to the leaves, and back again.

Plants Need Space

Plants need space to grow! Otherwise, their **roots** will get too crowded. This will force them to **compete** for nutrients and block one another's access to sunlight.

Plants Need Soil

Plants need soil to anchor their roots into the ground. Plants also use soil as a source of **nitrogen** and minerals. There are also bacteria and fungi that live in soil, close to the roots of plants, in order to help the nutrition move from the soil to the plants' roots. These bacteria and fungi are considered to be **symbiotic** with the plant roots, and require oxygen to carry out the necessary chemical reactions that keep themselves and plants alive.

Plants Need Light

What is the one thing that makes plants special? They are green! That green color in the leaves is actually from **chlorophyll**. Chlorophyll is a chemical that captures light and turns it into energy, which the plants need to grow. Without light, plants cannot make the **starches** and **sugars** that they need to build their own body parts.

Wait, so why don't WE need light in order to grow? Humans and other animals are called **heterotrophs** – we have to eat other living things for food. Plants, on the other hand, are **autotrophs**. They make their OWN food right inside their bodies using air, light, water, and soil. That process is called **photosynthesis** and it is unique to plants. Light also stimulates **germination**, which opens up the seed and allows the root and shoot to grow.

The following lesson allows students to explore the five needs of plants using the biodegradable Sunflower Microgreen Grow Kit as a scientific model of plant germination and growth.

Lesson 1: The Five Needs of Plants

Background

In this activity, students will learn about what plants need to grow by using the Sunflower Grow Kit as a model. They will experience the complete life cycle of a plant and have the opportunity to see the role that each of the five needs plays, demonstrating the concept of cause and effect.

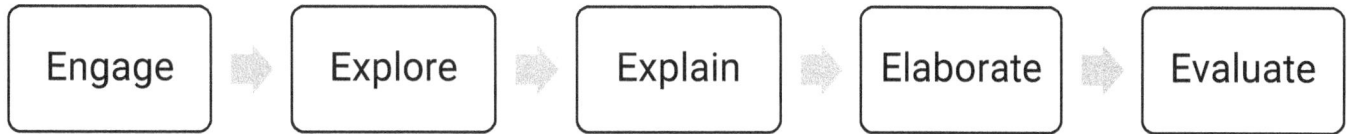

Engage ➡ Explore ➡ Explain ➡ Elaborate ➡ Evaluate

Performance Expectations
Students should be able to answer the following questions by the end of the lesson:
1. Where do seeds come from?
2. What is germination?
3. What does a seed need in order to grow?
4. What is the life cycle of a plant?
5. How do scientists learn about plants?

Prior Student Knowledge

Students must have prior knowledge of the concept of a "life cycle" or a "cycle" – the idea that the end of one process marks the beginning of another. Students must also be familiar with simple plant anatomy – leaves, stems, seeds, and roots. Bar graphs and ruler skills will also be explored in this lesson, so prior experience with these techniques is useful but not required.

Activities of this lesson by Academic Readiness, Learning Style, and English Proficiency

The following chart is included to help the educator determine how to deliver this lesson. Activities of the lesson are sorted by academic readiness, learning style, and starred if appropriate for ESL students.

		Academic Readiness	
		Struggling	**Accelerated**
Learning Style	**Visual**	Frayer Model Worksheet, *Cut-out Tray Signs for Labeling, *Coloring in the Plant Life Cycle worksheet, Make Like a Tree Worksheet	Frayer Model Worksheet, *Plant Life Cycle Fill in the Blanks
	Auditory	*Make Like a Tree: Act it Out Activity, My Microgreen Growth Log Book without measurements	My Microgreen Growth Log Book with measurements and graphing
	Kinesthetic	*Make Like a Tree: Act it Out Activity, *Grow kit procedure without 6 stations	*Make Like a Tree: Act it Out Activity, Grow kit procedure with the 6 stations each missing a component

Possible Preconceptions/Misconceptions

A possible misconception about plant growth is that plants get everything they need from the soil. In fact, most of the molecules for a plant's body comes from the air – carbon dioxide. Students may also believe that the seeds need to be buried deep into the soil. In fact, shallow planting is adequate for the grow kit as long as the seeds are kept moist.

Connections to Standards

Specific Learning Outcomes

Learning Outcome	NGSS Standard	NGSS Description
Plants come from seeds, and seeds come from fruits or flowers, depending on the type of plant.	4-LS1-1	Construct an argument that plants and animals have internal and external structures that function to support survival, growth, behavior, and reproduction.
	5-LS2-1	Develop a model to describe the movement of matter among plants, animals, decomposers, and the environment.
Name the five things a seed needs in order to grow: water, light, soil, space, and air.	4-LS1-1	Construct an argument that plants and animals have internal and external structures that function to support survival, growth, behavior, and reproduction.
	5-PS3-1	Use models to describe that energy in animals' food (used for body repair, growth, motion, and to maintain body warmth) was once energy from the sun.
	5-LS1-1	Support an argument that plants get the materials they need for growth chiefly from air and water.
Label the different stages of a plant's life cycle.	4-LS1-1	Construct an argument that plants and animals have internal and external structures that function to support survival, growth, behavior, and reproduction.
Reflect daily in science journals on observation of the growth of a plant, the way scientists collect data.	3-LS1-1.	Develop models to describe that organisms have unique and diverse life cycles but all have in common birth, growth, reproduction, and death.
	3-5-ETS1-3	Plan and carry out fair tests in which variables are controlled and failure points are considered to identify aspects of a model or prototype that can be improved.

Common Core Standards

ELA/Literacy
- Quote accurately from a text when explaining what the text says explicitly and when drawing inferences from the text.
- Integrate information from several texts on the same topic in order to write or speak about the subject knowledgeably.
- Write opinion pieces on topics or texts, supporting a point of view with reasons and information.

Mathematics
- Reason abstractly and quantitatively.
- Model with mathematics.
- Use appropriate tools strategically.
- Convert among different-sized standard measurement units within a given measurement system and use these conversions in solving multi-step, real world problems.

Next Generation Science Standards

SCIENCE & ENGINEERING PRACTICES:	DISCIPLINARY CORE IDEAS:	CROSSCUTTING CONCEPTS:
Developing and Using Models • Modeling in 3–5 builds on K–2 models and progresses to building and revising simple models and using models to represent events and design solutions. **Develop a model to describe phenomena.** • Science Models, Laws, Mechanisms, and Theories Explain Natural Phenomena • Science explanations describe the mechanisms for natural events. **Engaging in Argument from Evidence** • Engaging in argument from evidence in 3–5 builds on K–2 experiences and progresses to critiquing the scientific explanations or solutions proposed by peers by citing relevant evidence about the natural and designed world(s). • Construct an argument with evidence, data, and/or a model. • Support an argument with evidence, data, or a model.	**LS1.A: Structure and Function** • Plants and animals have both internal and external structures that serve various functions in growth, survival, behavior, and reproduction. **LS2.A: Interdependent Relationships in Ecosystems** **LS2.B: Cycles of Matter and Energy Transfer in Ecosystems** **PS3.D: Energy in Chemical Processes and Everyday Life** • The energy released [from] food was once energy from the sun that was captured by plants in the chemical process that forms plant matter (from air and water). **LS1.C: Organization for Matter and Energy Flow in Organisms** • Food provides animals with the materials they need for body repair, growth, and the energy they need to maintain body warmth and for motion. (secondary) • Plants acquire their material for growth chiefly from air and water.	**Systems and System Models** • A system can be described in terms of its components and their interactions. **Energy and Matter** • Energy can be transferred in various ways and between objects. • Matter is transported into, out of, and within systems.

ENGAGE

Access Prior Learning, Stimulate Interest, Generate Questions

Opening Activity: Make Like a Tree

Materials Needed

1. Celery (one fresh stalk, one wilted stalk)
2. Various pieces of dried fruit
3. Cups of water or other beverage
4. Some room in the classroom for students to stand up and move around.

Consider making flash cards or a poster of the boldfaced words to help the students remember the words used in the activity.

This activity can also be adapted to a worksheet instead of an active/verbal activity if desired. See the appendix for a sample worksheet.

Recommended Procedure

Ask the students to stand up to take part in this opening activity. Explain that we will be acting like plants to understand the five things that plants need to **germinate** and grow.

1. Plants Need Air

Ask the students to take a deep breath, and then exhale. Explain that we are breathing in **oxygen**, and breathing out **carbon dioxide**. Then explain that plants breathe as well, but in reverse! They breathe in the carbon dioxide we exhale, and we breathe the oxygen that they exhale. It is a team effort. They need air as much as we do!

2. Plants Need Water

Next, have students take a drink of water. Have students think about what would happen if they did not drink **water**. Plants need water to keep their **stems** and **leaves** crisp, but not too much water. Snap a piece of fresh celery in half, and then try the same with limp celery. Limp celery has too much water – it is rubbery. Then show the students the dried fruit – it has very little water. Ask the students if they notice a difference. Water also helps plants deliver **nutrients** around their bodies, like when we have juice or a sports drink.

3. Plants Need Space

Ask the students to stand very close together. Then have them stand far apart, spreading out their arms so that they are no longer touching another classmate. Ask them to explain which they would prefer if they were a plant, and why. Plants need space to grow! Otherwise, their **roots** will get crowded; they will **compete** for nutrients, and block one another's sunlight from getting to the leaves.

4. Plants Need Soil

Could you stand without the ground? No, of course not! Have students stand on one foot, and then on both feet. Ask them which they thought was easier. Ask if anyone has ever tried to run on sand at the beach. Was it easier or harder than walking on the sidewalk? Why? Plants need soil to anchor their roots into the ground. Plants also use the soil as a source of **nitrogen**. Soil also provides a home for **symbiotic** bacteria that help the plants get nutrients to their roots.

5. Plants Need Light

What is the one thing that makes plants special? They are green! That green color in the leaves is actually from **chlorophyll**. Chlorophyll is a chemical that captures light and turns it into energy that the plants need to grow. Without light, plants cannot make the **starches** and **sugars** that they need to build their own body parts.

Wait, so why don't WE need light in order to grow? Ask students to raise their hand if they know anybody who is green. [Wait for the laugh.] Humans and other animals are called **heterotrophs** – we have to eat other living things for food. Plants, on the other hand, are **autotrophs**. They make their OWN food right inside their bodies using air, light, water, and soil. That process is called **photosynthesis** and it is unique to plants. Pretty amazing!

EXPLORE

Lesson Description, Materials Needed, and Probing or Clarifying Questions:

Main Activity: Grow Your Greens

Materials Needed

1. Sunflower Grow Kit
   a. Seeds
   b. Soil
   c. Container
   d. Plastic baggies containing seeds and soil
   e. Instruction Card
2. A 6-ounce cup of water
3. A Spray bottle

Overnight Teacher Preparation: Remove the seeds from the seed packet and soak overnight (12-24 hours) before beginning the lesson.

Recommended Procedure

Follow the Grow-Kit Card Instructions. Students may work in pairs or in groups.
1. Add 6 tablespoons (3/8 cup or 3 fluid ounces – consider having the students figure out this conversion) of water to the bag of soil, close the bag, and mix well.

2. Pour the soil into the container and press lightly. You do not want to compact the soil too much, but you want it to be firm enough to support the seeds.
3. Spread the seeds over the soil and using the spray bottle, mist the seeds with water.
4. Place the container in the classroom window or another well-lit area.

STOP *You do not need to bury the seeds! Why not? Because many types of seeds actually need some light in order to germinate! It is better to plant too shallow than too deep.*

5. Spray the seeds thoroughly with water from a spray bottle. Place lid beneath the container to use as a drip tray.

STOP *Why do we leave the lid off? If the lid is closed, which of the five things will the seeds be missing? What do you think would happen?*

6. Repeat spraying 3 to 4 times per day. Students can take turns spraying their grow kit.
7. Once per day, students will draw and describe their observations on the "My Microgreen Log Book Worksheet" (pg. 12 – make multiple copies to create a booklet.).
8. Once the seeds have broken open and the sprouts have begun to emerge, proceed to step 9.

Daily Plant Care
9. After the sprouts first appear, add 2 tablespoons (1 fluid ounce) of water to the sprouts.
10. Repeat watering every two days, using about 2 tablespoons of water or a spray bottle to keep the seeds wet. Students may take turns watering.

Draw a picture of what the microgreens look like each day, with a caption under the drawing. Students should write what they observe and measure how tall the sprout is each day. Later, students can graph their results on the worksheet in the appendix.

Harvesting
11. When the microgreens are ready, harvest them with scissors or by pinching the stems one by one. Do not uproot the microgreens, simply cut them off at the surface of the soil.
12. You will know you are ready to harvest when the seeds fall off and the small rounded leaves (the cotyledon) are full, but the true leaves have not sprouted yet. (About 4-6 more days.)

STOP *What is a cotyledon? Why is it different from the true leaves? The cotyledon is actually the inner part of the seed that turns green after it pops out of the seed coat. It looks like a pair of leaves, but it isn't! The next pair of leaves that sprouts after the cotyledon are the true leaves. Those look a little different and more like what you would expect to see on the full sized plant. Leave a few in the container to keep growing or plant them outdoors or in a pot so that students can see the difference between the cotyledon and the leaves.*

13. Refrigerate the sprouts for up to 14 days after cutting (or eat them right there!)

EXPLAIN

Vocabulary Words and Concepts Defined

Germination – the process by which a plant grows from the seed, usually referring to the earliest stage where the seed coat opens, allowing the first root and shoot to emerge.

Carbon dioxide – Carbon dioxide is a gas that makes up less than 1% of the air we breathe, but plants rely on it as a source of carbon for their body parts. Sugars and starches are just long chains of carbon atoms and other molecules, so without carbon dioxide, plants have no building blocks!

Oxygen – Oxygen is a gas that makes up about 23% of the air we breathe. It is essential for life. Humans inhale oxygen while plants exhale oxygen.

Stems – The stems of plants are support structures but also act as veins and arteries of the plants. They allow nutrients and water to move between the stems and the leaves.

Cotyledon: an embryonic leaf in seed-bearing plants, one or more of which are the first "false leaves" to appear from a germinating seed.

Leaves – The leaves are like the solar panels of the plant. They capture the sun's energy and use it to make food. The first "true leaves" form just after the cotyledon.

Nutrients – Nutrients include any molecule that the plant needs to survive. In the case of plants, Carbon is a nutrient. So are various minerals like phosphorus and magnesium. Plants also need nitrogen. Fertilizer is a nitrogen-based nutrient.

Nitrogen – Nitrogen is a gas that makes up about 78% of the air we breathe. Nitrogen can also be in forms that are not gases. Bacteria in the soil help this process along, which then allows the plants to eat the nitrogen. Plants cannot actually breathe in nitrogen the way they do with carbon dioxide so bacteria need to help them!

Starch – Starches are just long chains of sugars, and sugars are molecules made of carbon, hydrogen, and oxygen.

Sugar – Sugars mentioned above, like sucrose, glucose, galactose, and lactose, are molecules made of carbon, hydrogen, and oxygen. They usually taste sweet, but some sugars are sweeter than others are. Table sugar is sucrose. However, plants make use of glucose, which is less sweet than table sugar.

Roots – The roots of plants are the part of the plant that is underground.

Chlorophyll – A green-colored molecule located in the leaves of plants that allows photosynthesis to take place. Chlorophyll molecules are zapped by the sun's energy to kick off the food-making process.

Photosynthesis – the way plants make food. Photosynthesis involves using the sun's light energy (photo) to make sugars (synthesis).

Heterotrophs – An organism that cannot make its own food so it has to eat other living things for food. The root "troph" means "to eat' and the word "hetero" means "other."

Autotrophs – The opposite of a heterotroph. An autotroph makes its own food with the right amount of energy input.

Symbiotic – A relationship between two living things that benefits both of them.

ELABORATE
Applications and Extensions

Remove Variables to Understand Their Purpose

For each group, one of the five needs of plants would be left out of the experiment, with the sixth group as the control with all components included. Students would be able to determine from real life experience how important each of the five needs are. Suggested groups are:

1. Set up the entire grow kit but either forget to water it or water it half as often (so it still grows, but not as well.)
2. Set up the entire grow kit without the soil, seeing if the seeds will still sprout by watering them in very little or no soil, in the bottom of the container.
3. Attempt to grow one of the grow kits in the dark and note the difference in results.
4. Attempt to grow one of the grow kits inside of a clear plastic container, so it still gets light, but has poor air flow
5. Plant all the seeds only to one side of the grow kit to crowd them and reduce the amount of space they have to flourish and note the differences in results.
6. Plant the kit per the instructions.

Let the Plants Reach Maturity for a Longer Term Experiment

Another elaboration on this lesson is to set aside a few of the unharvested microgreens to grow to full maturity somewhere on the school grounds or in a flowerpot. Students may wonder how long it will take to become a sunflower. Use this as an opportunity to explain where seeds come from in the first place.

EVALUATE
Formative and Summative Assessments

Formative Monitoring (Questioning / Discussion): Teacher will assess the students' learning using observational assessment of participation and answering of questions during group discussions.

Summative Assessment (Quiz / Project / Report): Teacher will assess the student's learning by ensuring that something has been recorded in their Microgreen Growth Log Book every day and that it accurately reflects what was going on with the microgreens at that time. Students may also graph the sprout height against the number of days the microgreens are growing and complete the other attached worksheets for class credit.

MAKE LIKE A TREE
An Introduction to the Five Needs of Plants

1. My life would be different without AIR because

    _____

    _____

    _____

    _____

2. My life would be different without the SUN because

    _____

    _____

    _____

    _____

3. My life would be different without THE GROUND because

    _____

    _____

    _____

    _____

4. My life would be different without WATER because

    _____

    _____

    _____

    _____

5. My life would be different without SPACE TO GROW because

    _____

    _____

    _____

    _____

DAY #	Height of Sprout: _____ inches or centimeters

What It Looked Like:

Who Watered?

DAY #	Height of Sprout: _____ inches or centimeters

What It Looked Like:

Who Watered?

DAY #	Height of Sprout: _____ inches or centimeters

What It Looked Like:

Who Watered?

DAY #	Height of Sprout: _____ inches or centimeters

What It Looked Like:

Who Watered?

To Teacher: Photocopy this page many times to make a booklet

Cut this sign out to label
each student's
container! (Optional)

Plant Name

———————————

Date Planted

———————————

Student or Group Name

———————————————

———————————————

Place This End into Soil to
Label Your Container

Plant Life Cycle: Fill in the Blanks

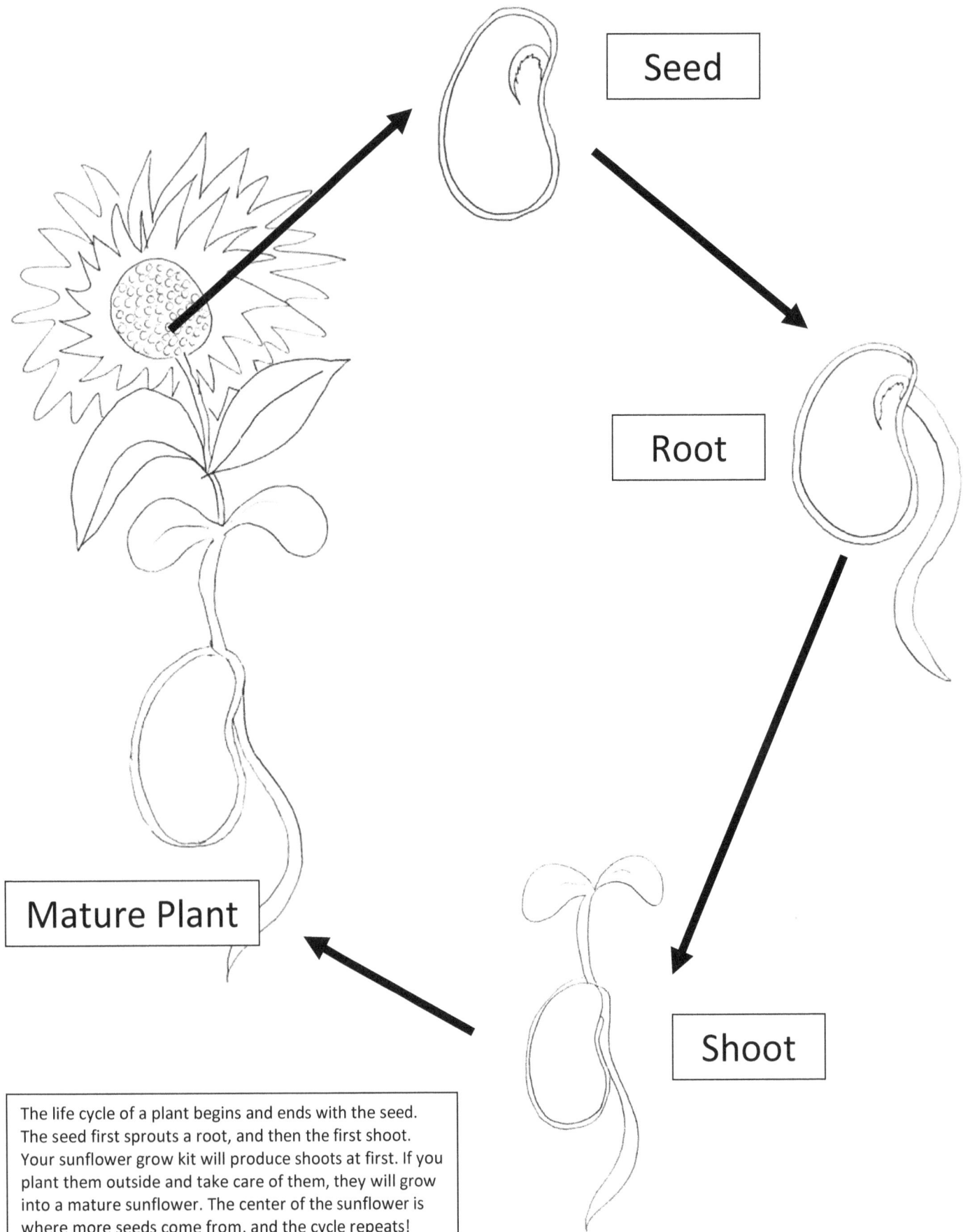

Seed

Root

Shoot

Mature Plant

The life cycle of a plant begins and ends with the seed. The seed first sprouts a root, and then the first shoot. Your sunflower grow kit will produce shoots at first. If you plant them outside and take care of them, they will grow into a mature sunflower. The center of the sunflower is where more seeds come from, and the cycle repeats!

14

Understanding Plant Vocabulary

Write the word in the center and fill in the information around it.

Examples

Definition

Word:

Opposites

Drawing

Lesson 2
Biodegradable Materials

In this activity, students will set up an experiment to determine and compare the biodegradability of different materials, including the Sunflower Grow Kit container, made of PLA (a plant -based plastic substitute). The experiment will simulate the conditions of biodegradation using hot water so students may see the results sooner than burying the materials in the ground.

Introduction to Biodegradable Plastics

The Plastic Problem

Plastic waste is a huge problem for the environment. Plastic is made from fossil fuels, which are non-renewable and take hundreds of years to break down in landfills. Even though we use most plastic products for a very short time, they will still be around long after their useful life, taking up space and even causing harm to wildlife.

What are Bioplastics?

Plastics manufacturers have begun to answer the call from society to make plastics that are still useful, but break down faster. The most familiar bioplastics are made from materials such as cornstarch and sold under such names as EverCorn™ and NatureWorks. The Sunflower Grow Kit container is made from NatureWorks, and the company states that it is guaranteed to decompose fully under composting conditions after 2-3 months.

How is this better than plastics based on fossil fuel? Corn is renewable. We can grow more if we need it. The cornstarch containers are made from a polymer called polylactic acid, or PLA. PLA is made by converting **starch** into lactic acid and then performing sophisticated chemical reactions that link all of the lactic acid molecules together in a chain, hence the name "poly-lactic-acid." ("Poly" means "many".) A **polymer** is an extremely large molecule -- a long chain of smaller units, like beads on a string. All plastic, even regular plastic, is a polymer. Regular plastic is made from fossil fuel derived units, while bioplastics are made from plant-derived units like **sugars**.

Biodegradable vs. Compostable

The difference between **biodegradable** and **compostable** plastic is subtle but important. Biodegradable means that the polymer will eventually break apart into smaller and smaller molecules. This could still take a long time and may leech harmful byproducts into the environment while doing so. Compostable is a special type of biodegradable, which means that the polymer breaks down in a relatively short time under composting conditions with its byproducts harmless to and indistinguishable from soil. It becomes **compost**.

The most important part of biodegradation is the role of microorganisms, like bacteria and fungi. They do the work of actually breaking down the materials. Scientists are still discovering types of bacteria and fungi that will eat almost anything, even oil and plastic! Still, biodegradation can take a long time, and anything we can do to make that job easier for these microorganisms will only improve our waste situation.

Factors Affecting the Rate of Biodegradation

- Water – Water is a solvent. It allows the chemical reactions carried out by the bacteria to do their work more efficiently, and it aids in dissolving the plastic.
- Pressure – Fossil fuels are broken down plant matter from millions of years ago, under pressure from the layers and layers of Earth above them. This is why they are considered

non-renewable – they would take longer than many generations of humans to make more because of the long timescale it takes plants to become oil.
- Time – Biodegradation takes time. The longer you wait, the more the material breaks down! Some materials break down in a few weeks, and others take millions of years.
- Heat – Higher temperatures allow chemical reactions carried out by the bacteria to proceed at a faster rate. That energy input also breaks apart the polymers directly.
- Bacteria – Bacteria are the primary drivers of biodegradation. Without them, biodegradation would not take place at all, or it would take place very slowly.
- Light – Ultraviolet light from the sun assists in breaking down polymers into their subunits.

Modeling Biodegradation

In this activity, biodegradation of some materials used takes many months to years. Attempting to see this in real time in the classroom would be unrealistic. In this case, we use hot water as a **simulation or model** of the energy input that breaks down materials in nature. This way, students will be able to witness a process similar to biodegradation in the classroom, on a time scale that is fast enough for engaging students and teaching the concept. It is important to make sure that students understand that hot water in a beaker is only a model of the process, and that the real process is much more complex.

In this experiment, it is important to note that the independent variables are time and the material type, and the dependent variable is the weight of the material being tested. Students may test plastics, metals, paper products, and anything else they choose. Everything else is kept equal across all of the tests (water temperature, water volume, and object size).

IMPORTANT! The polylactic acid (PLA) container is compostable only under industrial composting conditions. This is much different from backyard composting. Industrial composting uses machinery to finely chop the **feedstock** to make the biodegradation process more efficient. Industrial composting also reaches very high temperatures for very long periods of time. Therefore, you may find that the PLA container does not actually break down in this experiment. This is because PLA is technically a plastic, and plastics cannot be dissolved in water, even boiling. If they could, they would not be very useful to us! You may, however, see it warp and change shape.

So, while PLA is more environmentally friendly because it does not come from fossil fuels, dissolving the material in a laboratory setting would, just like regular plastic, still require strong solvents that are too dangerous to work with at home or in school.

Lesson 2: Biodegradable Materials

Background

In this activity, students will set up an experiment to determine and compare the biodegradability of different materials, including the Sunflower Grow Kit container, made of PLA (a plant -based plastic substitute). The experiment will simulate the conditions of biodegradation using hot water so students may see the results sooner than burying the materials in the ground.

Performance Expectation(s):

By the end of the activity, students should be able to:
1. Organize a group of items into categories
2. Carry out a simple experiment.
3. Understand that some materials break down faster than others do, and some not at all!
4. Explain the processes that might affect how quickly something breaks down
5. Make predictions about how biodegradable an untested material is
6. Graph results on a line graph of weight versus time to understand cause and effect.

Prior Student Knowledge:

This experiment explores the concept of biodegradability. Before this lesson, make sure students understand the meaning of the word "biodegradable." The experiment can be done in groups, with each group given the same or different items from the list below, or each group could be assigned two materials to compare. The grow kit PLA container should be included among those items.

Students should understand that water is a solvent. Students should also consider that the boiling water is supposed to simulate the much slower process of biodegradation in the natural environment. In the soil, heat, ultraviolet light, pressure, moisture, time, and microorganisms determine the true rate of biodegradation of materials.

Possible Preconceptions/Misconceptions

Students may not be aware that biodegradability is based on the activity of microorganisms. They may believe that things fall apart in nature over time without realizing the role that microorganisms play in that process. Students may also be unfamiliar with how scientific experiments are set up and may have difficulty with the graphing activity. Students may struggle to understand how the hot water simulates the process of biodegradation, so extra attention should be given to explaining that it is a model of a much more complex, natural process that can't easily be replicated in the classroom.

Activities of this lesson by Academic Readiness, Learning Style, and English Proficiency

The following chart is included to help the educator determine how to deliver this lesson. Activities of the lesson are sorted by academic readiness, learning style, and starred if appropriate for ESL students.

		Academic Readiness	
		Struggling	**Accelerated**
Learning Style	**Visual**	The Causes of Biodegradation, End of lesson questions asked as a worksheet	Line Graph Worksheet, Pros and Cons of Scientific Models
	Auditory	The end of lesson questions asked as a class discussion	Pros and Cons of Scientific Models as a class discussion
	Kinesthetic	*Categorizing materials into groups	Making predictions about how materials will biodegrade after categorizing them into groups

Connections to Standards

Specific Learning Outcomes

Learning Outcome	**NGSS Standard**	**NGSS Description**
Organize a group of items into categories	5-PS1-3	Make observations and measurements to identify materials based on their properties.
Carry out a simple experiment.	3-5-ETS1-3	Plan and carry out fair tests in which variables are controlled and failure points are considered to identify aspects of a model or prototype that can be improved.
Understand that some materials break down faster than others	4-ESS2-1	Make observations and/or measurements to provide evidence of the effects of weathering or the rate of erosion by water, ice, wind, or vegetation.
Explain what might affect how quickly something breaks down	4-ESS2-1	Make observations and/or measurements to provide evidence of the effects of weathering or the rate of erosion by water, ice, wind, or vegetation.
Make predictions about how biodegradable an untested material is	5-LS2-1	Develop a model to describe the movement of matter among plants, animals, decomposers, & the environment.
	5-ESS2-1	Develop a model using an example to describe ways the geosphere, biosphere, hydrosphere, & atmosphere interact.
Graph the results of an experiment on a line graph of weight vs. time to understand cause and effect.	5-ESS2-2	Reason abstractly and quantitatively. Model with mathematics.

Common Core Standards Connections

ELA/Literacy

- Quote accurately from a text when explaining what the text says explicitly and when drawing inferences from the text.
- Integrate information from several texts on the same topic in order to write or speak about the subject knowledgeably.

- Write opinion pieces on topics or texts, supporting a point of view with reasons and information.

Mathematics
- Reason abstractly and quantitatively.
- Model with mathematics.
- Use appropriate tools strategically.
- Convert among different-sized standard measurement units within a given measurement system (e.g., convert 5 cm to 0.05 m), and use these conversions in solving multi-step, real world problems.

Next Generation Science Standards

SCIENCE & ENGINEERING PRACTICES	DISCIPLINARY CORE IDEAS:	CROSSCUTTING CONCEPTS
Developing and Using Models • Modeling in 3–5 builds on K–2 models and progresses to building and revising simple models and using models to represent events and design solutions. **Planning and Carrying Out Investigations** • Planning and carrying out investigations to answer questions or test solutions to problems in 3–5 builds on K–2 experiences and progresses to include investigations that control variables and provide evidence to support explanations or design solutions. **Engaging in Argument from Evidence** • Construct an argument with evidence, data, and/or a model.	**LS2.A: Interdependent Relationships in Ecosystems** **LS2.B: Cycles of Matter and Energy Transfer in Ecosystems** **PS1.A: Structure and Properties of Matter** **ESS2.A: Earth Materials and Systems** **ESS2.E: Biogeology** **ETS1.B: Developing Possible Solutions**	**Systems and System Models** • A system can be described in terms of its components and their interactions. **Scale, Proportion, and Quantity** • Standard units are used to measure and describe physical quantities such as weight, time, temperature, and volume. **Cause and Effect** • Cause and effect relationships are routinely identified, tested, and used to explain change. **Patterns** • Patterns of change can be used to make predictions.

ENGAGE

Preparation and Introduction to Concepts

Explain "Biodegradable" to the class using the Causes of Biodegradability Chart

Gather the following suggested supplies and cut into 1x1 inch squares ahead of time.
- Styrofoam
- Plastic shopping bag
- Cardboard
- Copy Paper
- Newspaper

- Cereal Box Cardboard
- Fabric
- Leaf
- Aluminum foil
- Waxed paper
- Packing popcorn
- Plastic wrap
- A plastic take-out container
- A small piece of food

As a class, group the different materials into categories of the students' choice. Discuss why the categories were chosen.

EXPLORE

Lesson Description, Materials Needed, and Probing or Clarifying Questions:

It is assumed that before beginning this lesson, the previous lesson "The Five Needs of Plants" has been completed and students have harvested microgreens from their kits.

Materials Needed

1. The empty PLA grow kit container
2. 1-inch-by-1-inch pieces of the materials suggested in the previous section.
3. *Measurement Option 1:* Laminate an 8.5" x 11" letter-sized paper with a grid of 1/2 inch squares printed on it for estimating the size of the material as it breaks down.
4. *Measurement Option 2:* A scale with grams out to at least one decimal place
5. Colored marking pens, pencils, or crayons
6. Four borosilicate glass beakers or canning jars, 500mL or 1000mL size
7. A hot plate that can boil water
8. Scissors
9. Small Binder clips
10. Thin string or yarn of various colors

Recommended Procedure

1. Fill the four beakers with water and get the boiling started on the hot plates ahead of time.
2. It is probably best to have this set up at a front table away from the students.

STOP *Safety first! Only the teacher should be handling the boiling water.*

3. Group students into pairs, trios, or a group size that is reasonable for the class size. Each group will correspond to a color: Red, Yellow, Blue, Green, and White (string colors). These groups can reflect groups used in the previous lesson, "The Five Needs of Plants" where the grow kit was grown out and harvested.

4. After students have harvested their microgreens, have each group discard their soil.
5. Each group should select three material pieces in addition to their PLA container.

After selecting the three pieces, have students fill out the worksheet identifying each material. Save this worksheet because it will be used to collect data later.

6. Using the scissors, students should cut out a 1x1 inch piece of their grow container. The easiest place to take it is from the lid since it is flat. <u>*Safety tip: Snip off the corners of pieces. They can become sharp during the course of the experiment.*</u>
7. For each of the three pieces of material as well as the PLA square, have students (teacher can assist) clip the binder clip around the piece of material.
8. Students will next tie a string through the loops of the binder clip so that they are able to get their item out of the water for weighing or measurement without burning their hands.
9. Dip each piece of material into water to get it wet first. Weigh each piece of material with the binder clip and string attached to get an accurate weight. For the grid method, record the size of the object by itself. You will see why you laminated this – it gets water all over it!
   a. Record the baseline weight or size on the worksheet mentioned in Step 4a.
10. Students should approach the front table to add their pieces of material to the boiling water with the string hanging over the side of the beaker.
11. Begin timing 5 minutes. At 5-minute intervals up to 30 minutes, the teacher will lift all of the strings to remove the objects from the water at the same time. Students will approach the table to get their objects for weighing or sizing. Tare the scale and weigh. For the grid method, record the size compared to the 1/2 inch markings as it changes.

   ✓ *Record the weight or size of the object after 5 minutes.*
   ✓ *Record the weight or size of the object after 10 minutes.*
   ✓ *Record the weight or size of the object after 15 minutes.*
   ✓ *Record the weight or size of the object after 20 minutes.*
   ✓ *Record the weight or size of the object after 25 minutes.*
   ✓ *Record the weight or size of the object after 30 minutes.*

12. For either weight or size, graph the results with time on the x-axis and weight on the y-axis.
13. Return to the worksheet and identify the most biodegradable material based on the results of the experiment. See "Elaborate" for follow-up question ideas and extensions.

EXPLAIN

Concepts Explained and Vocabulary Defined

Biodegradable: The ability to be broken down in the natural environment, usually by bacteria or other microorganisms. There are bacteria in the world that eat just about anything! Eventually, everything biodegrades but some materials take much longer to be eaten than others.

The causes of biodegradation
- <u>Water</u> – Water is a solvent. It allows the chemical reactions carried out by the bacteria to do their work more efficiently, and it aids in dissolving the plastic.

- <u>Pressure</u> – Fossil fuels are broken down plant matter from millions of years ago, under pressure from the layers and layers of Earth above them. This is why they are considered non-renewable – they would take longer than many generations of humans to make more because of the long timescale it takes plants to become oil.
- <u>Time</u> – Biodegradation takes time. The longer you wait, the more the material breaks down! Some materials break down in a few weeks, and others take millions of years.
- <u>Heat</u> – Higher temperatures allow chemical reactions carried out by the bacteria to proceed at a faster rate. That energy input also breaks apart the polymers directly.
- <u>Bacteria</u> – Bacteria are the primary drivers of biodegradation. Without them, biodegradation would not take place at all, or it would take place very slowly.
- <u>Light</u> – Ultraviolet light from the sun assists in breaking down polymers into their subunits.

Independent Variable: The variable in an experiment that you change in order to see its effect. There are two independent variables in this experiment – time and the material type. We let time progress to see it's effect and we change the material type to see how it breaks down.

Dependent Variable: The variable in the experiment that is affected by the change you made. The dependent variable in this experiment is the weight of the material. We see how it's weight changes as it breaks down in the hot water over time.

Polymer: A molecule that is made up of a string of smaller molecules, like a string of beads. Plastic is a type of polymer and there are many different kinds of plastic, grouped by the type of "beads" in the chain.

Starch: A type of polymer that is made of **sugars** as the "beads" in the chain.

Metal: Metals are made of atoms on the periodic table. Some of them are pure, made of only one type of atom, like gold, aluminum, or tin. Others are mixtures of atoms, like steel.

Simulation or Scientific Model: A simulation or a model means to set up an experiment that is supposed to share certain characteristics of the real life scenario. This is done when it is impossible to do an experiment on the real life situation, or if it would take too much time to be realistic.

Compostable: A special type of biodegradable material that breaks down into products that are indistinguishable from soil.

Feedstock: The material that goes into the composting unit to be degraded as bacteria food! Consider this to be the "input" for the system.

Compost: Compost is considered an "output" of the system. It is what results when the feedstock breaks down. Compost is a kind of fertilizer; it contains nutrients necessary for plants to grow, like nitrogen, phosphorus, potassium, and magnesium.

ELABORATE

Applications and Extensions

Students may go outside and set up a long-term version of the experiment where they cut out a second set of squares to bury in the dirt. The class can check their objects periodically over several months to compare real-life biodegradation to the classroom simulation.

Students may also modify the experiment by measuring both the weight and the size changes of each object and discuss whether the weight or the size are better indicators of how much the object has broken down. This may vary by material tested.

Follow-up Questions for the Lesson
1. What were the independent variables?
2. What was the dependent variable?
3. Which materials were the most biodegradable?
4. Which materials were the least biodegradable?
5. Were the results from all the groups the same or different?
6. How were they different and why?
7. What are your conclusions for this experiment?
8. What would you do differently next time?
9. What variables affect biodegradability?
10. Why did we use hot water to simulate the conditions for biodegradation?
11. In what ways is a beaker of boiling water different from real biodegradation?
12. Did the PLA actually break down in the hot water? Why or why not?

EVALUATE

Formative and Summative Assessments

Formative Monitoring (Questioning / Discussion): Teacher will assess the students' learning using observational assessment of participation and answering of questions in the group discussions.

Summative Assessment (Quiz / Project / Report): Teacher will assess the students' learning using the My Data Collection Log and Line Graph worksheets.

ADDITIONAL INFORMATION

Troubleshooting, Online Demonstration

For a demonstration of how to do this experiment, with full-color pictures, please visit our website **http://www.growgreenspace.org/growkit** for a link to the instructions.

For troubleshooting advice, do not hesitate to contact **gina@growgreenspace.org** or visit our website for frequently asked questions.

Follow-up Questions

1. What was the independent variable? _____

2. What was the dependent variable? _____

3. Which materials were the most biodegradable?

   _____

   _____

4. Which materials were the least biodegradable?

   _____

   _____

5. Were the results from all the groups the same or different? _____

6. How were they different and why? _____

   _____

   _____

7. What are your conclusions for this experiment? _____

   _____

   _____

8. What would you do differently next time? _____

   _____

   _____

9. What variables affect biodegradability? _____

   _____

   _____

10. Why did we use hot water to simulate biodegradation?

    _____

    _____

    _____

11. In what ways is boiling water different from real biodegradation?

    _____

    _____

    _____

12. Did the PLA actually break down in the boiling water? Why or why not?

    _____

    _____

    _____

Make a Line Graph of Your Results
(One line per material that you test)

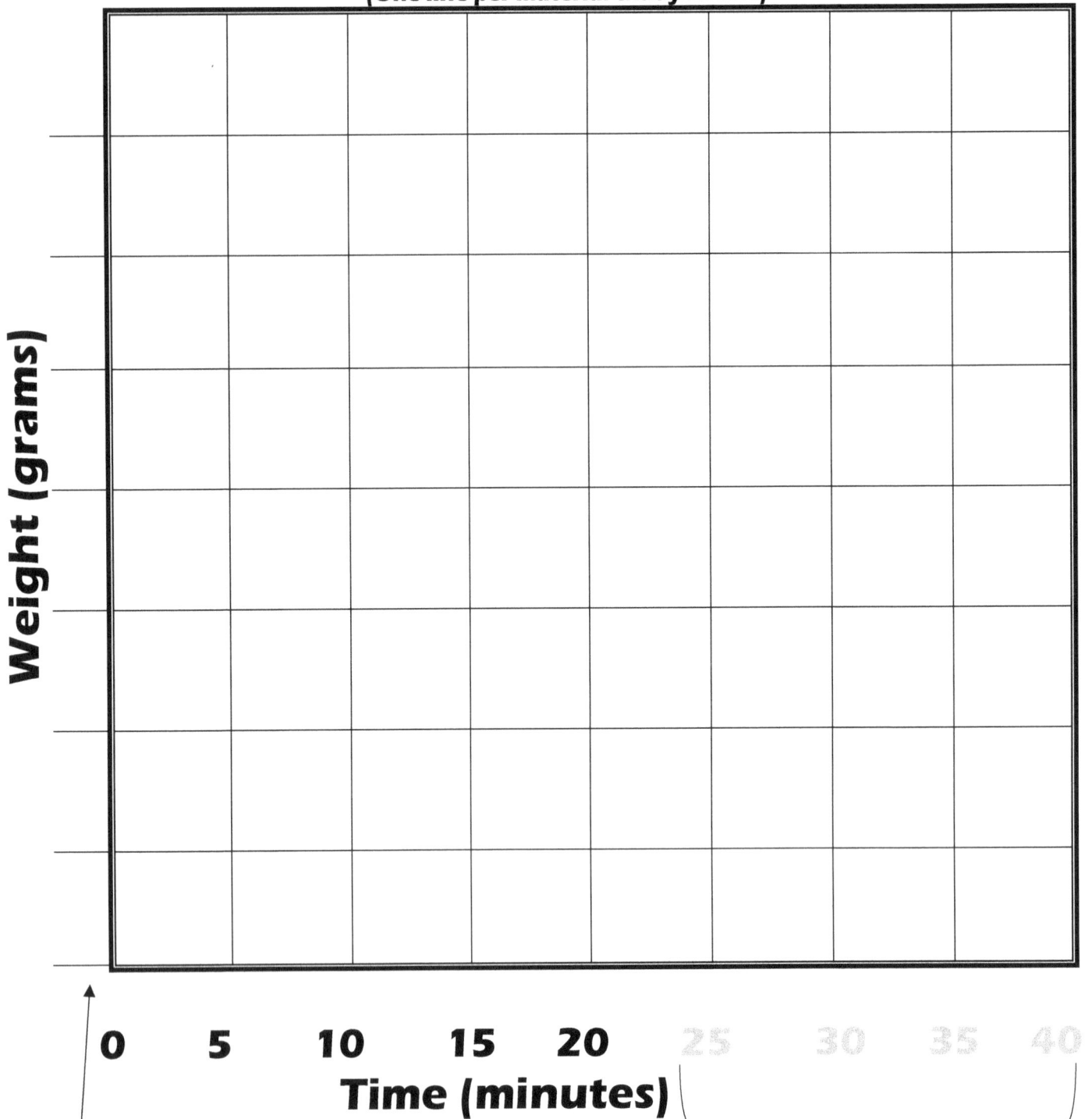

Weight (grams)

0   5   10   15   20   25   30   35   40

Time (minutes)

Set the Scale!
Number from 1 through the highest weight you got out of all your objects. Ask your teacher for help if you can't figure it out!

Make a Prediction!
What do you think the weight will be at these times based on what you've seen happening already?

28

My Data Collection Log

Material	What is its purpose?	Weight in grams			
		5 min	10 min	15 min	20 min

My Conclusions

_____

_____

_____

_____

_____

_____

Pros	Cons

Scientific Models

Similarities to real life	Differences from real life

Resource Guide

Further Reading for Educators

Bioplastics

Websites

- Sustainable Plastics | http://www.sustainableplastics.net
- Explain That Stuff, "Bioplastics" | http://www.explainthatstuff.com/bioplastics.html
- Everything You Need to Know About Bioplastics |
  https://www.creativemechanisms.com/blog/everything-you-need-to-know-about-bioplastics

Journal Articles

Harding KG, Gounden T, Pretorius S. "Biodegradable" Plastics: A Myth of Marketing? *Procedia Manuf*. 2017;7:106-110. doi:10.1016/j.promfg.2016.12.027.

Emadian SM, Onay TT, Demirel B. Biodegradation of bioplastics in natural environments. *Waste Manag*. 2017;59:526-536. doi:10.1016/j.wasman.2016.10.006.

Composting

Websites

- The Environmental Protection Agency's Compost Page on the Basics of Composting |
  https://www.epa.gov/recycle/composting-home
- Uncle Jim's Worm Farm and Everything You Need to Know to Start Worm Composting at
  Home | https://unclejimswormfarm.com/

Microgreens

Websites

- US Department of Agriculture's Agricultural Research Magazine on Microgreens, "Speciality
  Greens Pack a Nutritional Punch" | https://agresearchmag.ars.usda.gov/2014/jan/greens
- University of Florida IFAS Extension, "Microgreens, a New Specialty Crop." |
  http://edis.ifas.ufl.edu/hs1164

Journal Articles

Xiao Z, Lester GE, Luo Y, Wang Q. Assessment of vitamin and carotenoid concentrations of emerging food products: Edible microgreens. *J Agric Food Chem*. 2012;60(31):7644-7651. doi:10.1021/jf300459b.

Xiao Z, Codling EE, Luo Y, Nou X, Lester GE, Wang Q. Microgreens of Brassicaceae: Mineral composition and content of 30 varieties. *J Food Compos Anal*. 2016;49:87-93. doi:10.1016/j.jfca.2016.04.006.

www.ingramcontent.com/pod-product-compliance
Lightning Source LLC
Chambersburg PA
CBHW081233020426
42331CB00012B/3158